D1432806

WITHDRAWN

FEB _ _ 2015

Jefferson Twp Public Library
1031 Weldon Road
Oak Ridge, N.J. 07438
973-208-6244
www.jeffersonlibrary.net

The
WORST-CASE SCENARIO
Survival Handbook:

The
WORST-CASE SCENARIO
Survival Handbook:

Jefferson Twp. Public Library
1031 Weldon Road
Oak Ridge, NJ 07438
973-208-6244
www.jeffersonlibrary.net

By David Borgenicht and Justin Heimberg

Illustrated by Chuck Gonzales

A⁺
Smart Apple Media

A WORD OF WARNING: It's always important to keep safety in mind. If you're careless, even the tamest activities can result in injury. As such, all readers are urged to act with caution, ask for adult advice, obey all laws, and respect the rights of others when handling any Worst-Case Scenario.

Published by Smart Apple Media, an imprint of Black Rabbit Books
P.O. Box 3263, Mankato, Minnesota 56002
www.blackrabbitbooks.com

Copyright © 2015 Smart Apple Media. All rights reserved. No part of this book may be reproduced in any form without written permission from the publisher.

This library-bound edition is reprinted by arrangement with Chronicle Books, LLC, 680 Second Street, San Francisco, California 94107

First Published in the United States in 2009 by Chronicle Books LLC.

 A QUIRK PACKAGING BOOK.

Text and Illustratration © 2009 by Quirk Productions, Inc.
Worst-Case Scenario and The Worst-Case Scenario Survival Handbook are trademarks of Quirk Productions, Inc.

Book design by Lynne Yeamans.
Typeset in Adobe Garamond, Blockhead, and Imperfect.
Illustrations by Chuck Gonzales.
Library of Congress Cataloging-in-Publication Data
Borgenicht, David.
 The worst-case scenario survival handbook : extreme junior edition / David Borgenicht and Justin Heimberg.
    pages cm
 ISBN 978-1-59920-973-9
 1. Social skills in children--Juvenile literature. 2. Socialization--Juvenile literature.
 3. Children--Humor--Juvenile literature. I. Heimberg, Justin. II. Title.
 HQ783.B663 2015
 613.6'9--dc23
                                    2013037219

Printed in the United States at Corporate Graphics,
North Mankato, Minnesota, 2-2014, PO 1644
10 9 8 7 6 5 4 3 2 1

The publisher, packager, and authors disclaim any liability from any injury that may result from the use, proper or improper, of the information contained in this book.

CONTENTS

Welcome to Team Extreme

You may have heard the saying "If life hands you lemons, make lemonade." That's great, but what do you do when those lemons are being handed to you by a 400-pound (181-kg) gorilla? This guide will prepare you for just that sort of scenario, and it'll give you hundreds of other tips to help you become the ultimate extreme adventurer.

And when we say extreme, we mean *EXTREME!* In capital letters. And italics. With an exclamation point. Yes, the first day of school is *extremely* uncomfortable, and a wedgie from a bully can be *extremely* painful. But we're talking about a whole different level of *extreme.* We're talking pythons, tarantulas, sandstorms, piranhas, sharks, quicksand, elephant stampedes, mountain lions, tigers, and bears, oh my!

When faced with these kinds of extreme situations, extreme action must be taken. FAST! There's no time to sit down and draw a flow chart. No time to phone a friend or ask your parents for advice. It's all about *you*, and what *you* know, right then, right away.

But don't freak out. The information in this book spans the globe, across the seven continents, from ocean to desert to forest to tundra. No unsafe place is safe from our extreme survival know-how. So whether you're going on an adventure in Africa, the Arctic, or merely in your imagination, you're covered. Just stay calm. Surviving an extreme worst-case scenario is as easy as 1, 2, 3 . . . (OK, sometimes you might need 4, 5, 6.)

But even if you don't have plans to go on safari or explore the tundra any time soon, you'll still find this book packed with interesting (and sometimes surprising!) facts. Did you know, for example, that the most dangerous animal in Africa is actually the mosquito? Or that lightning really *can* strike the same place twice? And did you know that tarantulas can shoot their hairs like tiny darts? You *will* know after you read this guide.

Read, and dare we say, study up. Commit these tips to memory, because a good extreme adventurer is an informed extreme adventurer.

So turn the page and begin your initiation into Team Extreme. When you're done reading, you'll have everything you need to take on the world's worst (not to mention lots of cool information to impress your friends with). Good luck on your journeys.

Be safe. Be smart. Be extreme.

—David Borgenicht and Justin Heimberg

CHAPTER 1

How to Survive at Sea

How to Fend Off a Shark

Few images spark as much fear in swimmers as a shark fin slicing through the water. Never mind that deer kill 300 times more people a year than sharks! (See *Oh Deer!*, page 38.) But even though shark attacks are *very* rare, it's good to know what to do if Jaws drops in on your swim.

1 ## Stay calm.

This is sort of a given. It wouldn't be very good advice to tell you to panic and scream like a baby, would it? The point is, just because you see a shark does not mean it will attack. Signs a shark may be getting just a little deadly include it swimming in increasingly smaller circles and rubbing its belly against the seafloor.

2 ## Hit it!

If a shark comes at you, you have just one choice: Fight back. Fight dirty. Go for the shark's most sensitive spots: its eyes and gill openings. Punch, poke, and kick. This is a pro-wrestling match, and you're the bad guy.

3. A boxer never quits.

Keep on hitting the shark—jab it over and over in its sensitive spots. If you can convince your toothy opponent you're too much trouble, it may look elsewhere for its lunch. After all, you wouldn't want to eat a peanut butter and jelly sandwich that slapped you across the face, would you?

4. Get away.

Your best bet is to get on dry land, where Jaws can't follow (at least not before another million years of evolution). If you're in too deep (like if you're scuba diving), try hiding in weeds or against the seafloor, where it'll be harder for the shark to get to you.

Real or Ridiculous?

Which of these sharks are real?

a. Hammerhead Shark

b. Screwdriver Shark

c. Sawtooth Shark

d. Phillips-Head Screwdriver Shark

e. Staplermouth Shark

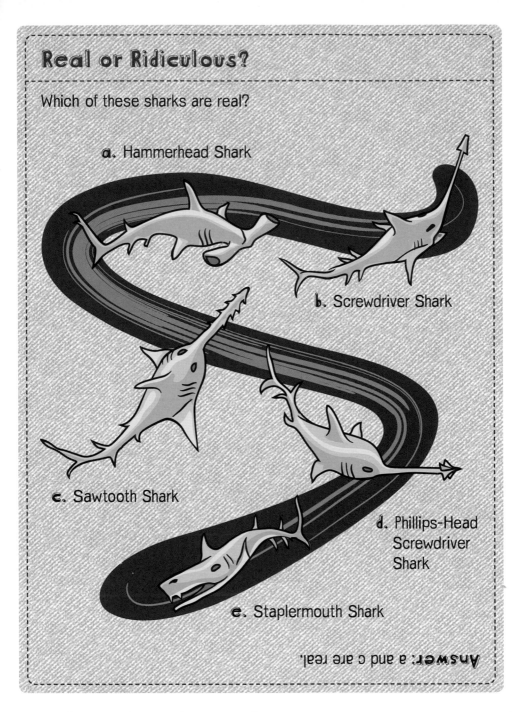

Answer: a and c are real.

How to Build a Raft After a Shipwreck

At first, the idea of being shipwrecked on a remote island seems pretty cool—endless days frolicking on the beach. Then again, there's no air conditioning or video games. Here's how to get back to the real world.

1 **Go logging.**

Clear a path into the interior of the island and find two logs about your height and ten logs about twice your height. OK, lumberjack, now lug those babies back toward the shore. Hey, no one said this was going to be easy.

2 **Live on the edge.**

Place the two short logs at the edge of the water at low tide. This is important: You wouldn't want to build the world's greatest raft, complete with swimming pool and mini golf, only to realize you can't get it in the water. Lay the longer logs on top of and across the shorter ones so they extend a bit past both short logs.

3   The rest is easy—*knot*!

Here's the hard part. You need to tie the logs together. Seaweed or vines are probably your best bet for string substitutes if you don't have actual string. Securely tie the logs together with long lengths of vine wrapped in figure eights and as many knots as you can.

4   Surf's up, ship out.

When the tide comes in, the water will flow under and around the raft. The raft will start to float, and you can push it out into the water. Now all you need to do is survive in the world's biggest wave pool (see *How to Survive When You're Adrift at Sea*, page 18). Good luck!

Island Inventions
(in Decreasing Order of Genius)

Surviving is all about being resourceful and creative. What would *you* make if you were stranded on a deserted island?

Tepee using logs
and parachute

Shiny coin fishing
lure and thorn hook

Palm leaf
water collector

Coconut basketball

Flounder hat

How to Survive When You're Adrift at Sea

If you're ever in a shipwreck, you'll need your wits, your strength, and your nerves of steel. Oh, and a lifeboat would help! Once you're adrift in the great deep blue, use these tips to steer yourself to safety.

1 ## Collect rainwater.

Supply your boat or raft with things that can function as containers: bottles, hollow coconuts, your World's Greatest Grandkid mug, anything. Let them sit in the rain to collect water. Then put lids on your containers (you can make lids out of whatever is handy) so you can store the water and avoid spills. Drink small sips, not big gulps, so your body can absorb the water.

2 ## No loose ends.

Tie your water containers to you or the boat to make sure you don't lose them. In fact, you may want to tie *yourself* to the boat so you don't lose *you*.

③ Don't work on your tan.

Act like a vampire at the beach and cover your skin as much as possible to avoid sunburn and sunstroke.

④ Land ho!

If you're in a busy area, you might be found by another ship. If not, keep your eye out for land. Even if you can't see land, there are signs you're nearing it:

- **Birds.** They'll fly back to an island at night, so follow their lead.
- **Driftwood.** If it's floating, land's approaching.
- **Murky water.** Muddy water means a river's mouth may be near—land could be just over the horizon.

5 Shore thing.

Choose a sandy beach over a more dangerous rocky or coral shore. If necessary, drift along the shore until you find the perfect place to land.

What's Your Worst Case?

Being stranded in a sea of snot?

or

Being stranded in a sea of vomit?

How to Avoid a Tsunami

Rearrange the letters in the word *tsunami,* and you can spell "I am nuts," which is what you are if you stay near the ocean when one of these monster waves approaches. Learn the warning signs so you can be far away when the ten-story-high waves come crashing down.

1 Hey, wasn't there an ocean here just now?
If the water level suddenly drops or rises for no clear reason, that's one sign of a coming tsunami. Or maybe a giant sea creature just took a big swallow. Either way, take the water movement as a cue to get your butt out of the water—and away from the beach altogether.

2 Water-quake!
Tsunamis are caused by underwater earthquakes. If you're on the shore and the ground begins to shake or you hear a low continuous roar, it's time to get going. Don't stop to grab your flippers.

3 **Up, up, and away.**

Get yourself off the beach and up to a high place, like the peak of the local mountain or the top floor of a tall building.

4 **Aah—aaah—*tsu*!!**

Like sneezes, the waves of a tsunami can keep on coming. Stay high and dry till things calm down. You don't want to end up soaked.

What Would You Do?

You are on a sailboat in a small harbor when you hear a loud roar and the sea level toward the shore seems to have dropped. What should you do?

a. Take your boat far into open water.

b. Stay where you are and lower the sail.

c. Sail near other boats—safety in numbers.

d. Abandon ship and dive to the magical undersea land of Zarnia, where the water nymphs and naiads can protect you.

Answer: a. Take your boat far into open water. Oftentimes, tsunamis are not even felt in deep water.

My Hero!

In 2004, a ten-year-old British girl named Tilly Smith, who had studied tsunamis in geography class, saw the receding ocean on Mai Khao Beach in northern Phuket, Thailand, and became a hero. She and her parents warned others on the beach, which was evacuated safely.

How to Treat a Jellyfish Sting

Imagine a mop made of stingers brushing across your body, and you'll have an idea of what it feels like to get stung by a jellyfish. The good news is that with the right recipe, you can at least lessen the zing of that sting.

1 Please pass the *salt* water.

Freshwater's the way to go when brushing your teeth, shampooing, and just about everything else. But with

a jellyfish sting, freshwater will actually make the sting feel worse, because it washes away salts that help lessen the sting. Rinse the sting with seawater.

② Break out the vinegar.

White vinegar, to be more specific. Why treat your wound like a salad? Because of *nematocysts*. Nematocysts are tiny structures in the cells of jellyfish that deliver the sting by firing tiny "darts" of venom. The acid in the vinegar deactivates these beasts. Bottom line: The vinegar takes the sting out. (No need to add croutons.)

③ Remove any tentacles.

Lift, don't scrape, any tentacles off using a stick or glove. If you scrape them off, you'll cause more stings to occur. You already have an entire Braille alphabet of stings on you, so there's no need for more.

④ To pee or not to pee? That is the question.

Some say *peeing* on a jellyfish sting will ease the pain. However, an Australian study showed that it actually caused more, not less, firing of nematocysts. So, it's best not to pee on yourself or a friend. What a relief!

How to Navigate by the Stars

Centuries ago, sailors used the stars to keep their ships on course at night. And guess what? Those stars are still twinkling, so you can use them to figure out which way is which, whether you're at sea or on land.

1 ## Take a dip.

The North Star (also known as Polaris) isn't the brightest star, so we use other stars to locate it, like the stars of the Big Dipper. You can't miss the Big Dipper—it looks like a big ladle that's scooping up some star soup.

2 ## Use your pointers.

Focus on the two stars that form the far end of the ladle's cup. These stars are called "pointers" because they point to the North Star. Just draw an imaginary line through the pointer stars and out across the sky, as shown on the right. The next star you'll see is the North Star.

③ Catch a falling North Star.

OK, stargazer. You've found the North Star. Now imagine that the North Star fell straight to the ground. Go find that fallen star. That's where North is. Now you can figure out south, east, and west—and head in the direction you want to go!

BE AWARE • If you're in the Southern Hemisphere, you can navigate by finding the Southern Cross, which is in the southern part of the sky. Either that, or just turn this page upside down and hope for the best.

Note: The Big Dipper might look like this, or it could be upside down in the sky. Look for it both ways!

Real or Ridiculous?

Which of these constellations are real?

a. Canes Venatici (Hunting Dogs)
b. Ursa Major (The Great Bear)
c. Pantus Cleanus (The Clean Slacks)
d. Castoris Bloatus (The Bloated Beaver)
e. Piscis Austrinus (The Southern Fish)

Answer: a, b, and e are real. Note: The Big Dipper is actually a part of the constellation Ursa Major. Can you spot it in the tail?

CHAPTER 2

How to Survive in the Mountains

How to Survive an Erupting Volcano

A volcanic eruption is basically a mountain throwing up. Things have been gurgling around inside for a while, and suddenly—SPEW!—a mess of liquid, solids, and gas is vomited out in a fiery mess. And this stuff really burns. Here's how to make sure that spew doesn't get on yew.

Look out—it's raining rocks.

When you think of an erupting volcano, you picture red hot lava flows dripping off a mountain like melting ice cream. But along with the rivers of fire, there are rocks being spit high into the air. If you're anywhere near a mountain that's blowing chunks, take cover if you can, and roll into a ball to protect your head.

Cool Volcano Words

aa (ah-ah): That is not a typo. And it's not you screaming either. *Aa* is a Hawaiian word for a type of lava with a rough surface of hard lava fragments.

caldera (call-DARE-uh): The crater formed by a volcanic explosion. (The mouth of the vomiting volcano.)

kipuka (kip-OOK-uh): A Hawaiian word for an area (like a hill) surrounded by lava flow, like an island in a sea of lava.

magma: Molten rock that is underground.

pillow lava: Blob-shaped formations of cooled lava that form when a lava flow enters the water.

2 Head for the hills!

Oh wait, the hills are on fire. That's not such a good idea. If the lava is headed your way, get out of its path as fast as you can. If you can put a ditch—or better yet, an entire valley—between you and the flow, so much the better.

3 Get inside.

Boiling lava on the ground, rocks raining from the sky? Time to seek shelter. Get inside—anywhere will do—as fast as you can, and try to get to a high story. Close all doors and windows. Don't open the door, not even if the lava knocks politely.

4 Up, up, and away.

Another nasty thing about a volcanic eruption is the mix of deadly gases that are belched forth. Carbon dioxide gas is the worst of 'em, and because it is denser than air, it will collect near the ground, so start climbing—stairs, furniture, whatever will keep your head above the murk.

How to Survive an Avalanche

Imagine being hit by a snowball as big as an ocean liner. That's what it feels like to be in an avalanche, and it's clearly a fight you want to avoid. But if Mother Nature throws the first snowball, staying on top of it (literally) is your best shot at riding to safety.

1 Brace yourself for impact.

If an avalanche is heading your way, don't let your jaw drop in shock—keep your mouth closed tight so you won't choke on snow. If you have ski poles, drop them (they can be dragged away, pulling you down), and crouch behind a tree or find shelter ASAP.

2 Ride the wave.

As the avalanche starts to close in around you, stay on top of the sliding snow by swimming in a freestyle (crawl) motion, using your arms and legs to keep you on the surface. It's the ultimate in bodysurfing.

BE AWARE • Never hike alone in avalanche country, and always carry an emergency beacon—a signaling device that will help rescuers find you if you are buried under snow.

3 When in doubt, spit.

If you end up in the middle of a snow cone, you need to find the surface. If you can't tell which end is up, dig a hole around you and spit. Your loogie will head downhill and give you an idea which way is up. Cool, huh?

4 Dig up.

Dig toward open air. Dig quickly, or someone may discover you in 2,000 years in the ice and say, "Wow, look at that perfectly preserved expression of panic!"

Avalanches to Imagine

Which kind of avalanche would you *least* like to be in?

- Soccer balls
- Thumbtacks
- Spray cheese
- Pudding
- Donuts
- Marbles
- Fingernail clippings
- Belly button lint
- Worms

How to Avoid a Bear Attack

For the most part, bears just want to live an easy country life. However, in certain situations, they can get testy. Like when they're protecting their cubs, feasting on deer, or when their houses have been broken into and vandalized by little blond girls who eat their porridge. Here's how to show bears the respect they deserve.

1 Sing out loud, sing out strong.

You don't want to freak out a bear by surprising it. As you hike, make noise by talking, singing a little forest karaoke, or by having a fascinating conversation with your echo. You could also fasten bells to your shoes or hat. Any sound will clue the bear in that you're coming, so *it* can choose to avoid *you*. That's the best-case scenario!

2 Keep your distance.

If you spot a bear, hold very still, and wait for the bear to go on its merry way. If you can, back away s-l-o-w-l-y to get more distance from the bear.

③ Know who you're dealing with.

Check if the bear is black or brown. Black bears are the most common in North America, but if you're in western North America, you might encounter a brown bear (like the grizzly or Kodiak). Coat colors can vary, though, so if you hike in a region with both black and brown bears, learn all the ways to tell the difference before you head out.

④ Play tricks.

If the bear is a black bear, and it's starting to charge you from afar, wave your arms and make noise—the bear will think you're bigger than you are and will back off. If it's a brown bear, curl up and lie still—playing dead will hopefully cause the bear to lose interest.

Oh Deer!

The most dangerous animal in America? The deer. That's right. Cute little Bambi is responsible for around 1.5 million car collisions in the Unites States alone every year, according to the Insurance Institute for Highway Safety. A total of 150 of these crashes are fatal for humans, and the horns-meeting-headlights destruction causes more than one billion dollars in property damage annually.

But the road isn't the only place a deer can be dangerous. As our neighborhoods start to take over the deer's homes, deer are losing their natural fear of people. During mating season (November–December), there have been an increasing number of deer attacks on humans by rambunctious bucks. With sharp antlers and club-like hooves, deer can be vicious.

Tell your parents to use the follow-ing tips when driving in deer country:

- Pay attention to deer-crossing signs and drive slowly when you see them.
- Be aware that deer are most active between the hours of 6 and 9 p.m.
- Do not attempt to sing a duet with a deer or any other woodland creature.

How to Survive a Lightning Storm on a Mountainside

Have you seen those "storm chasers" on TV? Those crazy folks who drive into the eyes of hurricanes? Do *not* try that at home! But even if you're not chasing storms, sometimes *they'll* chase *you*. Here's how to win this game of tag.

1 Stormwatch.

You love nature—if there are a few black clouds over-head, a little torrential downpour, so what? Lightning, however, is a different story, and you need to be aware of the signs when a storm is so close, you could be stuck:

- **A buzzing sound.** This is the sound of static electricity caused by tiny particles called electrons dancing about.
- **A sudden gravity-defying change in your hairstyle.** Your new 'do is the result of electricity in the air and in your hair!
- **A halo of light around people or trees.** No, you're not seeing things—well, actually you are,

but it's a real phenomenon known as "St. Elmo's Fire." The high voltage in the air reacts with the gas around objects and people to create the glow. Pretty cool.

② Do the math.

Arithmetic may be the last thing on your mind at a time like this, but a little division can help you figure out how close to you the storm is. When you see lightning, count the number of seconds until you hear thunder. Then divide by five. That's how far away the storm is in miles. Get to a safe place immediately if the thunder snaps,

crackles, or pops less than 30 seconds after the lightning. A storm even 6 miles away is within lightning-strike range. (It doesn't have to be raining on you for lightning to find you!)

3 Heavy metal?

Take off backpacks with metal frames and any jewelry. That navel piercing makes your belly button a bull's-eye. Tall things and metal objects are what lightning likes. That's why telephone poles aren't good hiking buddies.

Real or Ridiculous?

Which of the following are *real* effects of being struck by lightning? Which are *ridiculous*?

- You can turn the lights on and off by blinking.
- Your popcorn starts to pop before you put the bag in the microwave.
- Your hair is dark and curly (but it used to be blond and straight).
- You now sneeze the sound of thunder.
- You have a magnetic personality (literally).

Answer: Of course, *all* of these are ridiculous!

Gimme shelter (the right kind).

If you're in the forest and there are trees all around you, choose the shortest one and crouch under it, so you're the shortest thing in the area. If a tree has a lightning scar (usually a vertical patch that's been cut out of the tree or is covered in new, lighter bark), stay away—lightning *can* actually strike the same place twice. Stay away from isolated trees, metal fences, and bodies of water. All of these can attract lightning strikes.

How to Escape from a Mountain Lion

Ah, the peaceful sounds of the mountainside—birds calling, the wind in the trees, the low growl of a mountain lion—uh-oh. Here's how to stay safe in cougar country.

1 Don't be a copycat.

When you're near mountain lions (also called cougars and pumas), don't be a copycat; if you don't do like the big cats do, you'll be less likely to meet one. Don't hike at dusk or dawn (when they're on the prowl). If you see scratch marks on the trees, don't think, "Time to sharpen my fingernails." And definitely don't kill and eat a deer.

2 Run away? Not today.

Not to sound like the annoying lifeguard, but upon sighting a mountain lion, please do not run. If you run, it is likely to chase you. It's got four legs to your two. It's a lot faster than you. Don't find out the hard way.

Grow up.

You want to appear like a big ferocious animal so the lion doesn't think you're some easy-to-chomp little morsel. Look as big as you can. Stand up straight. Flex those muscles! Wave your arms over your head. Spread out your jacket like a king cobra. Bare your teeth and make some noise, y'all!

4 ## Back up.

If your tough-guy act doesn't petrify the puma, then you need to make the first move to break up this unhealthy relationship. Standing tall, slowly back away from the mountain lion.

5 ## Throw up.

This lion is not getting the hint; instead of walking away, he's stalking today. He's looking intently at you and crouching. You need to make it clear that you're not defenseless. Pick up some stones and toss them at the lion. Hard.

6 ## Protect your neck.

If the lion pounces, do not curl up to protect yourself. Mountain lions like to bite the back of the neck. Stay upright and maneuver to keep your neck away from the lion—kind of like how you'd avoid turning your back to a bully who likes to give wedgies. And yeah, a mountain lion neck bite is a *little* different from a wedgie, but you get the idea!

How to Go to the Bathroom in the Woods

Mountain lions, avalanches, volcanoes—all formidable foes. But what's the #1 wilderness worry? It's going #2.

1 ## Find your magic spot.

Pick a potty spot behind a tree or rock for privacy, far from the trail. This isn't a spectator sport. Stay at least 100 feet (30 m) away from any water source.

2 ## Dig a doo ditch.

Use a stick to dig a hole to bury your treasure. Make the hole deep enough to cover your "deposit."

3 ## Gather materials.

Find some nice soft leaves (unless you brought toilet paper) as wipes. Some hikers use pine cones, dry pine needles, or even a smooth "wiping stone." (Not something you'd want to keep for your rock garden or pet rock collection.)

BE AWARE • You should always make an informed decision on your brand of toilet foliage. Make sure you know what poison ivy looks like!

Poison Ivy

Cluster of three leaves
Grows as a vine or shrub

4 Bury your treasure.

Bury the leaves along with your poo. If you brought toilet paper, carry it out of the woods with you in a sealed plastic bag.

5 Wash your hands.

Wiping in the woods is an art that is rarely perfectly executed. So be sure to wash up. Wet your hands with water from a canteen or use a hand sanitizer.

The Circle of Life

Everyone has a favorite technique for fertilizing the soil. What's yours?

• The Invisible Chair
Press your back against a tree so your butt is suspended above the ground, as if you were sitting on an imaginary chair.

• The Standard Squat
Take a wide stance and crouch down over your homemade toilet. Note: This is only for those who have good balance.

• The Hanging Squat
Hold on to a tree in front of you, ideally one that bends (but doesn't break!). Place your feet near the base of the tree, bend your knees, and lean back.

• The Fallen Log
Hang your butt over the edge of a fallen log. There are two theories for the origin of the name of this method.

CHAPTER 3

How to Survive in the Desert

How to Get Along with Tarantulas

Relax. It's just a spider. A big hairy spider. With fangs. Fangs that can inject venom. Actually, you *can* relax. A tarantula is not that dangerous. Its venom causes nothing more than some minor swelling (unless you're allergic to it, which is rare). But why get that far?

The Tarantula Twist

Play poker.

If a tarantula makes a pit stop on you, find something like a stick or a rolled-up newspaper and gently poke your furry visitor. Poke at it the way you poke your fork at vegetables you don't want to eat. The big guy should mosey on off. Move along fella, nothing to see here.

2 Shake your booty.

If the poking isn't doing the trick, it's time to bounce up and down like an idiot. Stand up, bounce, and shake. So you look a little goofy. The tarantula is not one to judge. Who knows? The Tarantula Twist may become the next big dance craze.

Cool or Scary?

- The Goliath tarantula from South America has a body as big as a Chihuahua.
- Tarantulas actually run after their prey; they don't wait in a web.
- If forced to defend itself, a tarantula may flick tiny barbed hairs from its abdomen at its enemy.

How to Deal with a Scorpion

The scorpion, a relative of spiders, has eight legs and a stinger right at the end of its tail. But a wagging tail doesn't mean a scorpion is happy to see you. Do not lean over it and say, "Oh, wook at dat widdle guy waggin' his widdle tail!" When that stinger-capped tail uncurls like a party blower, the party's over.

1 Play hide and seek.

Comfy hiding spots, such as inside your shoes, under your bed linens, and under your pile of laundry are four-star accommodations to scorpions. Shake out your boots, bed linens, and clothes before using them. And at night, stuff your empty shoes so the scorpions don't tuck themselves in.

2 Leave stones unturned.

Resist turning over rocks or reaching into crevices. If you surprise a scorpion, the next surprise will be on you.

3 No shoes, you lose.

If you're camping in the desert, and you need to go to the bathroom at night, take the time to shake out and put on your shoes before venturing out. Scorpions are nocturnal (meaning they're active at night), and they will sting bare feet if they come their way.

> **BE AWARE** • On rare occasions, scorpions can be born with two tails. Double the pleasure!

How to Protect Yourself in a Sandstorm

Sandstorms can strike quickly and with little warning. One moment you're strolling along the dunes, enjoying the scenery, and the next, you're being blasted by a blizzard of sand grains. Here's how to ride out the storm.

1 **Seal your lips.**

The first thing to do is to cover your nose and mouth. Wet a bandanna, and, doing your best bandit imitation, wrap it around your face and nose. Resist the temptation to rob a train.

2 **Don't stare.**

Ever have something caught in your eye, like a gnat? It's torture. In a sandstorm, it's cool to be a four-eyes. If you have goggles or sunglasses, put them on. Turn your head away from the wind and close your eyes.

3 **Back that act up.**

Turn away from the wind. If you need to move toward the wind—say, back to your car or shelter—walk backward.

Super Sandstorms

Some of the biggest sandstorms in the world occur in the Sahara Desert of Africa, where they're called *haboobs*—Arabic for "strong wind." And "strong wind" is right! Gusts can create walls of sand 3,000 feet high—*twice* as tall as the Empire State Building!

How to Survive an Encounter with a Rattlesnake

Rattlesnakes, like all snakes, are cold-blooded and prefer hot climates. Not surprisingly, these venomous vipers, along with many other scary slitherers, call the desert home. Here's how to keep your cool if a rattler crosses your path.

1 Name that tune.

So, you're hiking a desert trail through the dunes when suddenly you find a large brown snake. You can check your field guide for a snake with a flat triangular head, thick body, and fangs like retractable needles. Or you can take your cue from the rattle at the end of its tail, which will probably start shaking and clacking. It's got a rattle, and it's a snake. Chances are you know what it is already.

> **BE AWARE** • Always stay on clear paths, so you can see what's underfoot!

② Don't get rattled.

So the rattler is still and coiled up, with a tail that sounds like it's playing the maracas. What does that rattling mean? Rattlesnakes don't come with warning labels, but if they did, this is what they'd say: Warning—if the snake is coiled and head is raised, get out of striking range. Also, if the rattle is a rockin', don't come a knockin'.

③ Freeze!

Don't move. Don't throw stones at the snake or poke it with a stick. Just back away. Give the rattler plenty of room—its striking distance can be half its overall length.

4 Fang you very much.

If you are bitten, stay calm, walk (don't run) to get medical help, and keep the bite above your heart if possible. Do not try to treat the bite yourself by bandaging it or putting anything on it—leave the rescue to the professionals. Though painful, rattler bites are rarely fatal.

Nanny, Nanny Boo-Boo!

Why does a snake stick out its tongue and hiss?

a. It's a warning to would-be attackers.

b. It thinks it's funny to taunt you.

c. It's feeding off particles in the air.

d. It uses its tongue to smell.

Answer: d. The forked tongue picks up odors from the air and touches them to openings in the snake's mouth. This is how a snake smells!

How to Find Water in the Desert

Out in the desert, there's no escaping the sun. Keeping hydrated is the only way to battle the constant thirst. When you've emptied your canteen, here's how to find some new, fresh water.

1 **Dry stream? I thought you said ice cream.**
Look for a dry creek bed—even if there is no water flowing, there may be some beneath the surface. Use a stick or your hands, and dig into the stream bottom to see if you find moist sand or water pooling. Dirt soup. Yummy.

2 **Trust your animal instincts.**
Animals need water too. If you follow an animal's tracks or call, you may be heading for the local wildlife water cooler. Of course, before getting a drink, you'll want to scope out the poolside for any predators.

Are Mirages Real?

A mirage is a real phenomenon that can make you think you're seeing a pool of water ahead of you in the desert. The sight you're seeing is absolutely real—you can even take a picture of it! But of course (sadly!), there's no real water there. This kind of mirage happens when the hot ground warms up the air above it, which causes rays of sunlight to bend so much that you actually see an image of the sky on the ground. This image can *look* like water and even *ripple* like water, but don't be fooled—there's not a drop to drink!

BE AWARE • You should always purify water you find in the desert (or anywhere in the wilderness) with a water filter or iodine tablets, or by boiling the water.

3 Show a "can dew" spirit.

Even in the desert, mornings following cold nights result in desert dew. (There's a bad name for a soda, huh?) You can scrape the dew drops off plants into your mouth. Hey, take what you can get.

How to Stop a Runaway Camel

Whether it's got one hump or two, a camel is the perfect desert transport. It can travel long distances with very little water and withstand the scorching desert sun. Though camels are easily trained, they're still prone to getting startled by loud noises and other surprises, so you'd better be prepared in case the one you're riding decides to make a run for it.

HOW TO RIDE A CAMEL

Before you can rein in a runaway, it's important to know how to ride a camel the right way.

1 You scratch its back . . .

It won't break yours. Rake the camel's coat before putting a saddle on. This removes any sticks or burrs that might be a real pain in the hump if stuck under the saddle. Feel free to gossip with the camel as you do its hair.

The Perfect Desert Vehicle

Paint job: A camel's thick coat reflects sunlight and insulates the body from the heat.

Headlights: Long eyelashes and—check this out—*sealable nostrils* help against blowing sand. There are times when we all wish we had sealable nostrils.

Fuel efficiency: A camel's organs and fatty humps allow it to go without water for long periods. Its pee comes out as thick as syrup and its poop is so dry it is used to light fires.

Wheels: Tough feet protect against hot sand.

❷ "Down, boy!"

It's a bad idea to take a running jump to mount a camel. Instead, trainers have taught camels to learn commands to make them kneel down. The trainer's Secret Word #1 will get the camel to crouch low enough that you can get on the hump.

❸ Don't get tossed.

After you utter Secret Word #2 for "up," the camel will stand. But brace yourself! The camel's backside goes up first and fast. Lean back, or you'll get a face full of sand.

❹ Gentle reins.

Riders use reins to steer a camel, just like they would with a horse. However, in the camel's case, the reins are attached to a peg in the nose. It's very punk rock. But be gentle. Think of how painful it is to yank a nose hair, and multiply that by ten.

❺ Sway with it.

A camel walks differently from a horse—the camel moves both right legs together, then both left legs, causing it to sway side to side. Sway with it, and you won't fall off.

HOW TO STOP A RUNAWAY CAMEL

1 Rein it in (sideways).

At speeds up to 40 miles per hour (64 kph), a runaway camel ride is no pony trot. You need to rein in your dashing dromedary. But don't pull back—that could snap the reins. Instead, pull the reins to one side. This will cause the camel to run in circles. Pull toward the side that the camel seems to prefer, not against it.

2 Hang on for your life.

Pretend you're in a rodeo, and while you may need to hang on for more than 8 seconds, it won't be *too* long. Get low, grip the camel with your legs, and hold onto the horn of the saddle tightly. The camel will eventually get tired of running in circles and realize it isn't really getting anywhere.

3 Make your perfect dismount.

The camel will sit when it gets tired, giving you a perfect chance to hop off. Tell the camel "good boy" for sitting. Give it a treat.

Spit Take

You may have heard that irritable camels will spit on people. Is it true? Yes and no. Camels rarely spit and are generally good-natured. However, if a camel feels threatened, it may spit at whatever is threatening it. Only, it's not really spit. It's worse. It's more like projectile vomit. A camel burps up the semi-digested food in its stomach into its mouth and then uses its lips to sling the goods. The result is a stream of stomach stuff that can cover your entire upper body!

CHAPTER 4

How to Survive in the Jungle

How to Cross Piranha-Infested Waters

What's worse than the worst day you've ever had at school? Spending a day in a school of piranhas. With their super-sharp teeth (which can bite through a steel fishhook!), a school of piranhas can strip the flesh from a fish or small animal in seconds. Here's how to stay off the menu.

1 Choose the non-piranha section of the restaurant, er, river.

The safest section of a river is away from the fishing docks. Docks where fish are cleaned are like fast-food restaurants for piranhas (complete with swim-through service and snappy meals).

FAST FACTS • Piranhas mostly live in South American rivers, like the rivers in the Amazon rain forest. People in the Amazon region have used piranhas' sharp teeth as tools.

② Flee the frenzy.

In a "feeding frenzy," piranhas will snap wildly at anything in reach. Even though you are unlikely to be the main course, don't let any parts of you become a side dish. Piranhas generally eat fish that are smaller than they are, so they'll only bite you if you get in the way.

③ Nighttime is the right time.

If you absolutely must cross a piranha-infested river, do it at night. The fish are less active, and if you awaken them, they're likely to swim away. Dawn is the worst time for a dip, as piranhas are hungriest in the morning.

What Would You Do?

You're bushwhacking in the Amazon in search of an ancient relic rumored to have mystical powers. You machete your way through the underbrush and come upon a river. The water is low since it's the height of the dry season. You're pretty scraped up from fighting through some thorns, and the water will feel good. Great time for a quick dip, right?

Answer: No chance, Crazy Pants. Piranhas can be dangerously hungry during the dry season, especially if they smell the blood from your wounds.

How to Escape the Grip of a Python

The world's largest snake, the python, can grow as long as a fire hose and as wide as a telephone pole. The reptilian giant is also a "constrictor," meaning it squeezes its catch in its coils until the pressure is too much to take. Here's how to avoid the Hug of Doom!

1 Be on the lookout.

Pythons are all about the ambush. If that branch is moving, get your patootie out of there. Pythons can strike suddenly. They can also stay underwater for 30 minutes.

2 Remain still.

If a python manages to give you a squeeze, relaxing your muscles may trick the snake into thinking you've been properly tenderized and are ready for consumption. He may loosen his grip. If so . . .

3 Go for the head.

Take off your reptilian body wrap. Just grab the head and unwrap it. Hey look, you shouldn't have tried it on in the first place.

What's Your Worst Case?

Sharing a sleeping bag with a python?

or

Taking a bath with a school of piranhas?

Who Would Win in a Fight—
an Alligator or a Python?

In 2005, a 13-foot (4-m) python and a 6-foot (2-m) alligator were found in an unusual position. The lifeless alligator was discovered sticking out from a tear in the equally lifeless snake's body. The snake probably thought it had won the battle after it swallowed the gator. However, it's not over till it's over, and unfortunately, in the end, it was over for both of them.

How to Escape from Quicksand

How many times have you been walking to school when BAM!, you suddenly stumble into a pit of quicksand? OK, so maybe quicksand isn't as common in daily life as cartoons seem to indicate. But if you're walking around the right (or wrong) riverbank, you just may encounter that rare substance that's created when water mixes with sand but doesn't form clay. Which makes it extra sticky and possible to sink into—like a big bowl of earth pudding!

1 **Walk softly and carry a big stick.**

If you're in quicksand country, bring a pole. The pole will help you if you get stuck. Try not to step anywhere that looks suspicious, like onto a sand-topped puddle or in the hole by that sign that says "quicksand."

2 **If you start to sink, lay the pole on top of the quicksand.**

Think of the pole as one of those foam-noodle-floaty things at the pool. Moving slowly, wiggle your back onto the "noodle" and slowly spread your arms and legs. Chill out until you start to float.

> **BE AWARE** • Always move slowly in quicksand. Thrashing around will tire you out and puts you at risk of inhaling sand, which can suffocate you.

3 **Float, don't flap.**

OK, so you forgot your pole. Don't panic: Your body is less dense than quicksand, so if you can relax, you will eventually begin to float. If you have a heavy backpack, shrug it off—anything that makes you heavy will make you sink.

How to Deal with an Angry Gorilla

There's a reason for the expression "to go ape"—a gorilla will scream, beat his chest, and bare his teeth when upset. Of course, it's all just a big show to look tough and assert the gorilla's rank in the group. To stay safe, you need to learn your role.

① Let's get ready to humble!

Gorillas are usually pretty peaceful—unless you're threatening them. So swallow your pride and let the gorilla win the staring contest. Stay quiet and keep your arms to your side, so he doesn't think you're testing his dominance.

② Don't call his bluff.

A gorilla may make a "bluff charge" to intimidate you. Well, be intimidated. If you're nose-to-nose with a 400-pound (181-kg) gorilla, make yourself small and act afraid. If he thinks you got his point, he'll let you off easy.

3 Offer groom service.

So you've just been charged by a giant ape. Caressing the mad monkey's fur probably seems like odd advice. In this case, however, the ape may take the hair care as a nonthreatening gesture, because lower-ranked gorillas will groom the head ape. In other words, if you can't beat 'em, groom 'em.

How to Remove a Leech

In the warm shallows of jungle pools lurks a little blood-sucker that loves to latch onto unsuspecting swimmers like you. Here's how to avoid being a leech's juice box.

1 ## Don't start in the middle.

When you find a leech stuck on you, resist the urge to just grab the leech in the middle and pull. The leech is lip-locked on your arm in not one, but two places! Playing tug-of-war with your own body is a game no one wins.

Leech Anatomy

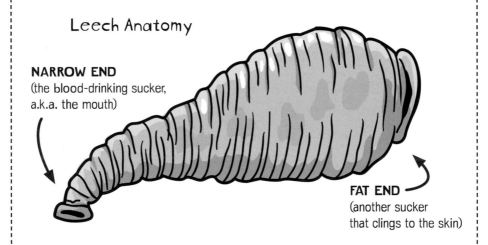

NARROW END
(the blood-drinking sucker,
a.k.a. the mouth)

FAT END
(another sucker
that clings to the skin)

What Would You Do?

Which of these methods are other ways of getting leeches off you?

- Salt
- Heat
- Insect repellent

Answer: None of them. These irritants will cause the leech to throw up into the bite, which can spread bacteria and cause infection.

2 Nail the leech.

Look for the small end of the leech—this is the mouth. Put your fingernail on your skin next to the leech, but not directly on it. Push against it sideways to break the seal.

3 So long, sucker!

Now push away the big end, while flicking at the mouth so it doesn't reattach. Fling the leech away, shaking it off your finger like an unwanted booger.

How to Catch Fish Without a Rod

Anybody can catch a fish with a motorboat, a fancy rod, and a state-of-the-art lure. The test of a true fishing master is whether you can catch a fish with nothing but the clothes on your back. Literally.

1 ## Make the frame for a net.

Find a young plant that splits into two branches, like the one shown on the right. It should be about as long as your leg. Bend the two branches toward each other and tie them together to make a circle.

2 ## Take the shirt off your back.

And your front. Don't forget your arms. In fact, take the shirt off completely! After you take off your shirt, tie a knot in the shirt below the armpits. Then tie the shirt to the sides of the net frame. Voilà, a net!

3 Stay out of the sun.

This is about catching fish, not rays. Fish like the shadowy places near the edges of the water, so that's your target area. Once you find the right spot, it's time to . . .

4 Net the surf.

When you swipe your homemade net through the pool, water should flow through the shirt, but fish will be caught.

How to Build a Shelter in the Rain Forest

With a name like "rain forest," it's probably going to rain in this forest—a lot. Which means that if you're lost here, you need to find (or make) some cover fast.

1 Location. Location. Location.

High and dry ground is ideal. Look for a clearing. Stay away from any swampy or low-lying spot, a.k.a. the mosquito breeding ground. And don't pick a spot under a coconut tree or a tree with any dead limbs, or else more than raindrops may fall on your head.

2 Lean on me.

Sticks and stones *can* protect your bones. Find a sturdy fallen tree trunk or a rock. Lean some thick branches and sticks at an angle against the fallen tree. This is why this sort of shelter is called a "lean-to." Crawl under it to make sure you have enough room to fit (your lean-to shouldn't be too-lean).

3 Seal it up.

Fill in all the holes with lots of large leaves and moss. Pile it on! You don't want any leaks. Hang a "Do Not Disturb" sign on the side of your shelter, so the jungle critters will leave you alone.

The Rain Forest by the Numbers

- The Amazon rain forest alone produces 20 percent of Earth's oxygen.
- More than 3,000 fruits are found in rain forests.
- Some experts believe we are losing 50,000 plant species a year from the destruction of the rain forest.

Other Shelters

The lean-to is just one easy shelter to make. There are loads of others to choose from depending on your circumstances.

The Dry Inn

If you have a poncho and rope, you can use it, instead of the leaves, as siding.

The Swamp Bunk

If you can't find a site away from the swamp, then you need to elevate your game with a covered, raised bed made from four trees and lots of brush.

The A-Frame

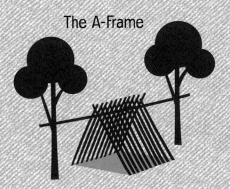

This is like a lean-to with two sides. Take a long log and balance it on a tree stump or rock. Then follow directions for a lean-to on both sides.

The Fantasy Fort

Who says rain forest living can't be posh? Just fly in an architect and some builders and make your abode a tad less humble. Star-gazing deck optional.

CHAPTER 5

How to Survive in the Arctic

How to Avoid a Polar Bear Attack

Here's the problem with polar bears: They have no natural predators, so they have little fear. This means they're not afraid of humans. All the more reason to watch your tushy on the tundra!

1 **If the bear doesn't see you, keep it that way.** Don't try to get a closer look or a better picture. Stay downwind of the bear, so it doesn't catch your funky odor. No offense.

2 **If the bear sees you, show you're only human.** If you see the bear standing, sniffing, or taking notice of you, let the bear know you're human by talking and waving your arms. If you're in a group, everybody should do this. Make a commotion. Have a dance contest.

Real or Ridiculous?

a. Polar bears have clear hair, not white hair. The hair *looks* white because it reflects light.

b. Some polar bears in Antarctica have black hair.

c. Polar bears have webbed front feet.

d. Polar bears have been known to make snowman-like structures and rub their backs against them.

e. Under their fur, polar bears have spotted skin.

f. Polar bears have taste buds on their toes.

Answer: a and c are real. Choice b was doubly ridiculous— there *are* no polar bears in Antarctica.

3 Stand your ground.

If the bear charges, should you jump in the water? No good. Polar bears are great swimmers. Hit the ice? No dice. Polar bears are quite the speed skaters. And in the snow, forget about it. Your only chance is to pollute the atmosphere and increase global warming, thereby making these beasts extinct. Just kidding. If the bear *does* attack, you and the group all need to attack back. Hopefully the bear will retreat, giving you enough space to then leave the area.

How to Survive Falling Through the Ice

Let's say you're walking on ice. (Which you shouldn't do.) Then let's say you walk onto *very thin* ice. (Which clearly you shouldn't do. *Dude, what the heck is wrong with you?!*) It's too late now. You've fallen in—but the good news is, you *can* get out.

1   Inhale. Exhale. Repeat.

Guess what? The water is going to be cold. As in shockingly, gaspingly cold. Try not to hyperventilate; stay calm. Tread water.

2   Remember where you came from.

Chances are you just walked away from the strongest ice. So turn to face the direction you came from. Look for your foolish footprints or a landmark like a tree or building to locate your point of origin.

3   Elbows out.

Get your elbows on the ice and hoist yourself up but not completely out of the water. You just gained a few pounds

How to Rescue Someone Else Who Fell Through the Ice

If someone else breaks the ice, don't jump in, too. Instead of becoming a second ice cube, coach them out. If they can't do it, throw them a rope, hockey stick, or even a long branch. Just don't reach with your hands, or the panicked person might pull you in!

with your "liquid diet," so let the water weight drain from your clothes before trying to pull yourself up.

4 **Go kicking and screaming.**

Kick your feet as if you're swimming to propel yourself forward as you pull yourself up onto the ice.

5 **Roll on.**

When you get out, do not stand up. Instead, roll away. This spreads your weight out over the ice and makes you less likely to fall through for a second time. And since you've already been introduced to the frigid water, there's no need to break the ice again.

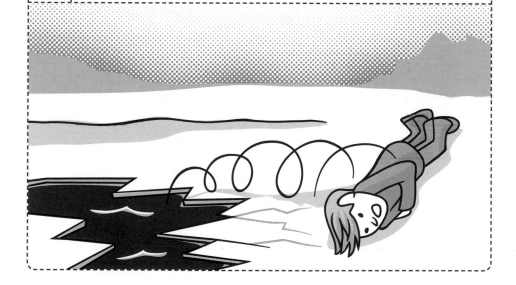

How to Deal with a Charging Moose

A moose is a lot like a Ferrari. It's shiny, sleek, and glamorous. OK, maybe not. But like a Ferrari, a moose can go from being completely still to moving very fast in a matter of seconds, bowling over anything in its way. Including you.

1 Dog-gone it.

To a moose, your dog looks a lot like a wolf. And a wolf is no friend to a moose. If you and Fido meet up with a moose, a) the dog is going to get upset and bark, b) the moose will think it has to defend itself, and c) the dog will then run back to its master. Which means, d) you are about to come face-to-face with an angry moose. So the moral of the story is: Don't bring your doggy on a hike in moose territory!

2 Give it an escape route.

Make sure the moose has a place to run other than over you. Generally a moose isn't looking to butt heads with you, and it will take a clear path if it has one.

Doodie Calls!

The Talkeetna Moose Dropping Festival is an annual celebration that has taken place in Talkeetna, Alaska, for more than 30 years. Varnished, numbered moose turds are dropped onto a target from a helicopter. People are given raffle numbers that correspond to the numbers on the turds. The closest turd to the target wins!

Moose Body Language

ears up

"Hm, what is that
all about?"

hair up

"I don't like you.
I think I'll knock you over."

"Would you like to join
me for tea?" (rare)

3 ## Speak "Moose."

The moose may look at you with its ears up. If so, you can back away from the merely curious moose. If the moose lowers its head and the hair on the back of its neck stands up, then you need to start worrying.

4 ## Olé? No way!

If the moose charges, don't act like a matador. The bull of the north has a mighty set of antlers. Get behind something solid and stay as still as a pill until the moose has passed. In fact, stay put until the moose has left the area, resettled, and started a new life as an accountant.

How to Make Emergency Snowshoes

Why get exhausted and risk frostbite slogging through deep snow when you can make a pair of snowshoes and walk right on top of the snow surface? All you need is a pair of tree branches and a little string. Here's how to get your kicks on the snow.

1 Branch out.

You're shopping in Old Man Winter's shoe store, so the selection is limited. Look for two tree branches about 2 feet (.6 m) long. As far as style goes, you want branches with lots of little branches and green needles on them. It's all the rage on the tundra.

2 Step on it.

Time to try on your new shoes. Step on your gathered branches. About a hand's length of branch should stick out in front of your foot. The rest of the bushy part should be around and behind your foot.

3 Tie it up.

You'll need string. Good thing you brought some for that Arctic String Convention. If not, you might be able to use plant roots, or there may be a drawstring on your bag or coat that you can repurpose.

a) Tie one end of the string to the front of the branch.

b) Lace the string through the front holes of your shoe.

c) Tie the other end of the string securely to the branch.

4 Make them yours.

Carve or mark your new shoes with whatever symbols or stripes designate your favorite shoe brand.

Pick Your Kicks!

Which of the styles below is your best bet for snowshoeing?

The Fir Flop

The Pine Pump

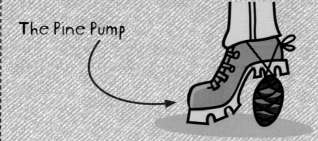

The Beaver Boots

Answer: The Fir Flop. You want lots of little branches so your weight is spread out and you don't sink, like you could with a heel.

How to Build a Snow Cave

So you're camping out in the wintry wilderness, when a sudden gust of wind sends your tent off for a solo hang glide. You need a new shelter fast, or you'll soon be a snow angel. Here's how to stay warm and dry even when surrounded by snow and ice.

1 Find the right spot.

Look for a steep-ish slope with a buildup of snow that's soft enough to shovel but hard enough to pack together.

2 Dig it.

Every ice fortress needs a door. Dig an entrance tunnel straight into the slope about 3 feet (1 m) deep. Next, carve the main chamber in and upward from the end of the tunnel. Keep the chamber floor flat and make the ceiling domed. The entrance tunnel must be lower than the main chamber. Otherwise, snow could be blown or fall through the tunnel into the chamber.

Make it holy.

When finished with the main chamber, poke a ventilation hole though the roof. This will ensure you have enough air to breathe, and you'll be thanking yourself if your fellow snow-caver lets one rip in the night.

> **FAST FACT** • The Yupik Eskimos have more then 20 words for snow, including *muruaneq* (soft deep snow), *natquik* (drifting snow), and *kanevvluk* (fine snow particles). They do not have a word for snow that isn't deep enough to cancel school, though.

How to Survive If Stranded on an Iceberg

No matter how you got *on* this floating chunk of ice, here's how to make the best of it—and how to get off.

1 Build on your 'berg.

You need shelter. You can build a trench (a long hole covered by blocks of ice) or, if you see an extended stay in your future, build a snow cave (see page 99)— icebergs are almost always covered in snow.

2 Snow + sun = water.

The surface of an iceberg is made mostly of freshwater, so you can drink to your heart's desire. Put the snow or ice in a container and let the sun beat down on it. Eating snow is not the same as drinking water (eating uses your body's energy, sapping you of much-needed strength), so fully melt the snow first. As a last resort, scrape at the top ice to make your own personal snow cone. Flavor: plain.

3 Go fish.

In general, a human can go three days without water and three weeks without food. That's a theory you don't want to test. End your hunger strike as soon as you can. Make a fishing rod out of anything you can. If necessary, hunt sea birds with ice balls.

4 Catch my drift?

In Antarctica, icebergs drift clockwise around the South Pole. Keep your eye out for ships and weather stations. In the Arctic, the currents flow east to west. You may drift to populated areas near Greenland. Of course, this ride will take a few months, so you'll have time to decorate your mobile home.

Real or Ridiculous?

Nature is a master ice sculptor. Scientists classify icebergs with different names, depending on their shape. All the icebergs in the world are monitored so that another *Titanic* disaster can't occur!

Which of these iceberg shapes are works of nature and which are not?

Punch bowl

Tabular

Dome

Tubular

Wedge

Globe

Answer: Tabular, dome, and wedge are real.

CHAPTER 6

How to Survive on Safari

How to Dress for Success on Safari

When a typical day on safari in East Africa may include meeting with lions, crocodiles, and elephants, looking fashionable may not be a top priority. But pick your clothing carefully: It's worth the effort to sport the right duds for your trip.

1 Be an onion.

This isn't about smelling bad or making people cry—this is about dressing in layers. You might be thinking, "It's gonna be steamin'!" Well, you're half right. It *will* be hot during the day. But night is a different story—believe it or not, it can get pretty cold in the African savannah.

2 Don't forget PJs.

In this case, PJs stand for "pull-over jackets." You'll want a warm jacket if you plan to be out or camp at night. Pack layers so you can control your temperature.

Extreme Makeover: Safari Edition

Before

Uncovered

Bright

Tight

Uncomfortable

After

Shady

Loose

Khaki

Layers

Zipper

Comfortable

3 ## Hang loose.

Tight clothes are a bad idea. You'll often need to cover your whole body to protect against mosquito bites and sunburn, and loose clothes will keep you cooler in the heat. And cotton has a way of getting wet and staying wet, so wear fabrics that dry quickly next to your skin instead.

4 ## Accessorize.

Protect your head with a wide-brimmed hat, sunglasses, and some sunblock. Cover your feet in sturdy, comfortable walking shoes. Better yet, wear special hiking boots or lightweight, quick-drying shoes with thick soles.

5 ## Go khaki, not wacky.

Leave the Hawaiian shirt at home. Blending in with your environment is the goal, and khaki is ideal. Bright colors can alarm animals.

> **FAST FACT •** The color blue can attract the tsetse fly, which carries a toxin that can cause the illness sleeping sickness, which causes fever, headaches, and joint pain, in addition to sleepiness.

Safari, So Good

Safari means "journey" in the African language of Swahili. Safaris used to be hunting trips, but these days, going on safari usually means traveling to a nature reserve in eastern or southern Africa, riding around in a car, and taking lots of pictures.

Safari-goers often search for the "Big Five" animals, but there are plenty of other great animals to see beyond these big shots. A short list is below, along with their Swahili names (which are pronounced just like they're spelled, for the most part).

Lion	simba	
Elephant	tembo	
Rhino	kifaru	
Leopard	chui	(pronounced "chewy")
Buffalo	nyati	
Giraffe	twiga	
Hippo	kiboko	
Cheetah	duma	
Zebra	punda milia	
Gazelle	swara	
Hyena	fisi	

The Big Five

How to Track Animals

Tracking is a crucial wilderness survival skill. Keep your eyes open for the signs an animal leaves, and you'll be able to avoid any predators and find the animals you *do* want to see when you're on safari.

1 Dust for prints.

Look for prints where impressions may be left, such as along streams or in dusty areas. Know the characteristic footprints of the critters you're interested in:

- Four toes per foot suggests dog or cat family.
- Elongated prints may be from the hoofs of a gazelle or giraffe.
- Comma-shaped prints might be a warthog or wild pig.

2 Be a poop-snooper.

Animals leave behind more than just footprints. Keep your eyes peeled for poop along the trail. The scoop on poop: If the animal is an herbivore (a vegetarian), it will leave round pellets. If the animal is a carnivore (meat-eater), its leavings will be long and tapered. It's your doodie, er, duty to track.

3 Watch their diets.

Knowing what comes out of an animal is important, but so is understanding what goes in. You gotta know what your animals like to munch on. Wildebeests eat the tops of grasses, while zebras mow their lawns down to the roots. Skilled trackers can even recognize the patterns of teeth marks on shrubs and bushes!

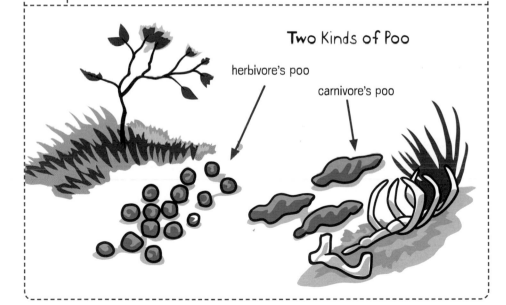

Two Kinds of Poo

herbivore's poo

carnivore's poo

How to Survive the Deadliest Animal in Africa

What do you think is the deadliest African animal? Go ahead, guess. The lion? The rhino? Wrong. The deadliest animal in Africa is no bigger than your fingernail. It's the mosquito. In Africa, mosquitoes can carry malaria, which kills up to two million people a year, so you want to be utterly repulsive to mosquitoes in Africa (or anywhere else where malaria is present). Here's how to get these pests to bug off.

① Be as repulsive as possible.

Get an insect repellent with the chemical DEET. Spray it on your clothes and skin as directed.

> **FAST FACT** • Only female mosquitoes suck blood—they need it for their eggs. Both males and females eat flower nectar and other sweet-smelling foods.

② Don't smell.

Avoid using hairspray, perfume, or other scented items that could smell sweet and attract the pests. If you smell like flowers or fruit, they'll think you're food.

③ Don't show skin.

At night, when mosquitoes are most active, cover your body from head to toe. Sleep in rooms with screened windows or under mosquito nets.

> **DID YOU KNOW?** • A small donation (as little as $10) can help a family in Africa get mosquito nets. If you want to help, just search online for organizations that take donations.

How to Escape from a Crocodile

How do you tell the difference between a crocodile and an alligator? Here's a rule of thumb: A crocodile has a long, narrow, V-shaped snout, while the alligator's snout is wide and U-shaped. Here's another rule of thumb: Never get close enough to be able to tell the difference.

1 Don't go it alone.

Never swim or boat by yourself in waters that are home to crocodiles. To a croc, a solo swimmer looks like a tasty treat, but a group of people just looks like trouble. Stay with your buddies.

2 Surrr-prise! *Not.*

If caught off-guard, a croc may attack on instinct. So if you suspect there could be one nearby, slap the water, shout, do impressions, sing your favorite song, whatever! Just make some noise.

③ Give it some space.

Crocodiles and alligators have been known to jump well out of the water to snag prey that thought it was safe to chill on low-hanging tree branches. If you see one, stay at least 20 feet (6 m) away from the water.

20 feet
(6 m)

4 **Do not feed the animals, please.**

Feeding crocs can cause them to get over their fear of humans.

5 **Get out of the croc-pot.**

Both crocs and gators have two sets of eyelids. They have a pair of clear inner lids that function as natural goggles and allow them to see perfectly underwater. Still think you're a match for Old Four-Eyes in the water? Consider this: Crocs have "skin sensors" that can sense vibrations when something enters the water. Bottom line: If you even suspect there's a crocodile around, get out of the water yesterday!

6 Run!

If you spot a croc on land, run. Run fast. Run straight. Run far.

3 Myths About Crocodiles and Gators

Myth #1: **They're slow.** A large croc can run 10 mph (16 kph), which is probably about the same speed you can run. Do the math. Actually you don't have time. Just run.

Myth #2: **You should run in zigzags.** This idea stems from the idea that crocs can only see straight ahead, so they'll lose sight of you if you zig and zag all over the place. However, you're better off running away any way you can. The more distance you can put between you and the croc, the better.

Myth #3: **Crocs like to chase people.** Actually, they're not like lions. They don't like to chase down their prey. They're way too cool for that. They're lurkers. They lie low before attacking.

How to Survive an Elephant Stampede

Sure, elephants may look big, clumsy, and slow, but they can actually run faster than 25 mph (40 kph). Their speed and strength makes elephants the linebackers of the Animal Kingdom. And while a herd of charging pachyderms can be scary, stay calm. Do the wrong thing, and you'll soon be elephant toe-cheese.

1 ## Take cover.

Running's not an option—the elephants will just catch up. Instead, find a sturdy structure to get into. Of course, there aren't always a whole lot of sturdy structures on the African plains. So . . .

2 ## Grab a trunk.

Of a tree, not an elephant! If you're a skilled tree-climber, you might be in luck. Elephants, even in a frenzied stampede, will try to avoid trees. Grab a branch and hoist yourself up, staying close to the trunk. If you can't climb a tree, huddle close to the tree trunk. *Be* the tree trunk.

3 Get down.

This might sound crazy, but if all else fails, lie down. Unless it sees you as a threat, an elephant is unlikely to step on you. If you stay standing, you run a higher risk of getting shish-kebab'ed on an elephant's tusk.

Do not grab an elephant trunk.

What's Your Worst Case?

Being sneezed on or Falling in a pile of
by an elephant? fresh elephant poop?

How to Survive a Charging Rhinoceros

The black rhino has a horn on its face and a chip on his shoulder. If one lowers its horny head and snorts at you, it's got goring you on its mind. You don't want to be on the receiving end of the charge from an animal that weighs more than a ton. Here's how to avoid it entirely.

1 ## Tree up, don't tee up.

At 30 mph (48 kph), a charging rhino is not outrunnable. If one comes at you, climb a tree. Make sure you get higher than the horn can reach, or you're just teeing yourself up for the rhino.

2 ## Scrub-a-dub-dub.

If you can't get to a tree, the next best thing is thick, scrubby brush. Get as far into the bush as you can. Don't worry, your panic will keep you from feeling the pricks of those sharp thorns. Better a thorn than a horn.

3 ## Opposites don't always attract.

Once you have avoided the charge, run in the opposite direction the rhino is running. These big boys don't like to turn around, so once they get going in one direction they're unlikely to reverse course. It's not a bullfight; you just need to avoid that first charge.

Real or Ridiculous?

The jolly-looking hippopotamus is actually one of the most deadly animals in Africa. Hippos are known for being aggressive when humans enter their territory, and they get particularly riled up when their path to water is blocked, as they spend most of their time underwater (even though they're mammals). Can you tell which of these hippo activities are real and which are ridiculous?

a. Hungry, hungry hippos have been known to tear full-grown crocodiles in half.

b. Hippos eat rocks to help them sink in the water.

c. A hippo is capable of jumping 2 feet (60 cm) in the air.

d. A hippo might fall asleep right in the water—and stay underwater for as long as five minutes before surfacing to breathe, all without waking up.

e. Baby hippos are born underwater, then they swim to the surface for air.

f. Hippos spin their tails to spread their poo, to mark their territory.

Answer: a, d, e, and f are true.

Appendix

HOW TO TELL DIRECTION WITHOUT A COMPASS

The Stick Shadow Method

1. Stand a stick up in the ground.
2. Mark the tip of the shadow of the stick.
3. Mark it again 15 minutes later.
4. Draw an imaginary line from the first line to the second. The line points east.

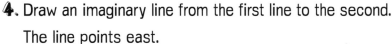

The Watch and Learn Method

1. Hold your watch so that the hour hand points directly at the sun.
2. Imagine a line halfway between the hour hand and the 12. That line will be pointing south.

OTHER WAYS TO TELL DIRECTION

- Most moss grows on the north side of trees.
- Spiderwebs are often built on the south side.
- Clouds often travel west to east.

Appendix

HOW TO SIGNAL FOR HELP

Third Time's the Charm

A series of three is the universal call for distress. If you have a whistle, blow it three times to call for help. If you have three pieces of bright material (a tent, poncho, tarp, etc.), set them side by side in a clearing so they can be seen by a plane flying by. Three rock piles will work as well.

Steer the Mirror

On sunny days, you can signal for help with a mirror or anything shiny that reflects light.

Appendix

FIELD GUIDE TO EXTREME FOODS

While on your travels, you are likely to encounter some pretty extreme foods. Know what they'll taste like before you take a bite with this handy chart.

Place	Food	What It Tastes Like
Ecuador	Guinea pig	Chicken
China	Turtle shell gelatin	Bitter cola
Tibet	Yak butter tea	Oily, salty tea with sour milk
Shanghai	Duck heads	Chewy chicken
Egypt	Camel	Grainy and fatty beef
Philippines	Sautéed crickets	Crunchy, buttery chewy morsels

Place	Food	What It Tastes Like
Hong Kong	Snake soup	Chicken broth with fish
Cambodia	Deep-fried spider	Crab with gooey black juice
Scandinavia	Lutefisk (air-dried whitefish prepared with lye)	Soapy, fishy gelatin
Morocco	Pigeon pie	Chicken pot pie
Mexico	Corn fungus	Mushrooms on the cob
France	Pâté (spreadable liver)	Wet cat food
Scotland	Haggis (sheep stomach lining stuffed with minced organ meats)	Wet cat food mixed with oatmeal, served in a balloon. (Do not eat the balloon.)
Your House	Fried chicken	Guinea pig, duck heads

Appendix

FOREIGN EMERGENCY PHRASES

Brazil (Portuguese)
Do those fish have teeth?
Aqueles peixes têm dentes?
a-KEH-les PEH-shehs teng DEHN-ch.

Kenya and other parts of Africa (Swahili)
Excuse me, there seems to be a large lion behind me.
Kubwa simba nyuma mimi.
CUB-wuh SIHM-buh NYOO-muh ME-ME.

Norway (Norwegian)
I'm sure that ice is safe to walk on.
Jeg er sikker på at den isen er trygg å gå på.
Yay ehr SEEK-er poh at dehn EE-sen ehr treeg oh goh poh.

Indonesia (Indonesian)
Look out! There's an orangutan behind that tree—maybe he wants your banana!
Awas! Ada orangutan* di belakang pohon itu—mungkin dia mau pisang kamu!
Ah-WAHS! Ah-dah ore-AHNG-oo-tahn dee beh-LAH-kahng poe-hone EE-too—MOONG-kin DEE-ah mao PEE-song KAH-moo!

* The Indonesian word *orangutan* means "person of the forest" (*orang* = person; *hutan* = forest).

About the Experts

These experts reviewed all the tips in this handbook and offered their extremely good advice. Consider them the coaches of Team Extreme!

"Mountain Mel" Deweese has more than 30 years of worldwide experience teaching survival skills. His work has spanned the globe, from the Arctic to the tropics, and he has dealt with animals of all sorts. He has shared wilderness survival skill knowledge with more than 100,000 students around the world and continues to do so through his Web site, www.youwillsurvive.com.

John Lindner is the director of the "Wilderness Survival School" for The Colorado Mountain Club, and he runs the "Snow Survival School" for Safety-One International, Inc. A former instructor for Denver Public Schools and the Community College of Denver, John has taught mountaineering and survival training for almost 30 years.

Charles Maciejewski has a degree in Adventure Education and has worked at Outward Bound, the Bronx Expeditionary Learning High School, and the Kurt Hahn Expeditionary Learning School. He has planned numerous urban and wilderness expeditions with students and trained teachers on doing work in nature. He loves the natural world, cycling, and snowboarding.

About the Authors

David Borgenicht is a writer, editor, publisher, and the coauthor of all the books in the Worst-Case Scenario Survival Handbook series. He has been known to float on quicksand, overpack while on safari, and employ "the standard squat" (see page 48). He lives in Philadelphia.

Justin Heimberg defines the word *extreme*. He is extremely cautious and wary. He is an extreme sleeper and an extreme television watcher. On the rare occasion when Justin is not being extreme, he writes books and films. He lives in an extreme suburb in Maryland.

About the Illustrator

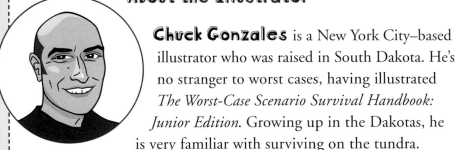

Chuck Gonzales is a New York City–based illustrator who was raised in South Dakota. He's no stranger to worst cases, having illustrated *The Worst-Case Scenario Survival Handbook: Junior Edition*. Growing up in the Dakotas, he is very familiar with surviving on the tundra.